DISCLAIMER

If you have had any form or accident, please do seek medical advice to ensure you are physically fit before riding. Riding is a risk sport and the author takes no responsibility, whatsoever, for any accident, injury, loss or damage to anyone or anything arising from riding or handling any horse or from practicing any of the methods set out herein.

I HOPE IT RAINS…

The confidence manual for the nervous rider. Practical, realistic advice to help overcome your fear and deal effectively with your anxiety whilst making small but positive steps to achieve your goals and enjoy riding your horse.

FOREWORD

As an adult you have learned that you need to avoid getting hurt or being put out of action, not least because you know it's unpleasant, but on a practical level, the bills must be paid and the daily chores must be done. With age supposedly comes wisdom and as a result, you almost certainly have a different approach from a child learning to ride. Kids, from my experience, watching my nephew and others at Pony Club, seem to just get on with it, gallop about, fall off, then bounce back on. They learn by doing, falling, getting back on and repeating, a lot! Miraculously, they don't seem to be hurt or phased by these mishaps. Covered in grass stains or sand from the school, off they go again on naughty little ponies determined to unseat their riders at any opportunity. As an adult, this is not usually the case. We have developed much greater levels of responsibility, self-preservation and an awareness of consequences. It's no wonder we have nerves when we are out of our comfort zone!

Knowing what it felt like to be nervous and learning to break down the problem to cope with and overcome the negative feelings was the foundation of this book, albeit at the time I had no clue it would ever be something that I would write down beyond my own lists and self-set goals. Over a relatively short time, time I managed to go from being a complete, but fairly "gung ho" novice to a very upset nervous wreck, then back to a stubbornly determined novice. By taking small steps, with hours and hours of dogged practice and latterly with good tuition, I became an accom-

plished rider. I am by no means saying I am the best rider in the world but I have seen the coin from both sides and know fear as well as I do fun and success on a horse. I was like my 9 year old Pony Club nephew when I started to ride. I didn't really get in any bad situations (luck not judgement) and I was really enjoying riding, despite not learning until I was 22. At the beginning I was fairly clueless but I had no negative pre-conceptions of what a horse/rider can do or the pickles and scrapes that they can find themselves in. I had rose-tinted spectacles and was happy with it that way! However, this brave, 'horses are nothing but good fun' atti-tude came crashing down around me when I bought my first horse, just a few years after beginning riding. I had ridden regularly, several times a week and I desperately wanted a horse of my own.

My first horse, the one that I actually bought with my hard earned cash rather than a loan horse or pay per ride was, ironically, the one that nearly destroyed my riding confi-dence for good. He was very handsome but most unsuitable for the level of rider I was as the time. My dream ended up being a nightmare in a matter of months. He took me apart, decked me at every opportunity on fields, roads or in the school. I was out of my depth and to make matters worse, he was not a forgiving creature and went out of his way to be naughty! He tried his best to remove my friend who I had asked to help me after weeks of disaster and at the time I had no real clue why she stayed on him and I would end up face first in the sand. The answer to this was simply SKILL. She had it, I didn't. She was not a brave woman particularly but she was more COMPETENT than me at that time. I was forced to realise this (which did take some time to sink in) and it really upset me if I am honest but being stubborn I was determined to keep going. I was going to the stables every day (literally hoping it would rain to give me a reason not to have to ride) and reluctantly getting on him knowing full

well at some point he would catapult me off on to the floor or in to the fence. I was young, fit, tenacious and not easily scared, but over time the constant poundings he dished out took their toll.

It was at this point I reached rock bottom and was almost crippled with fear. I was devastated. I never stopped caring for him but I would literally ask him why he hated me so much when all I wanted to do was have some fun and give him everything he needed in return! He never answered me, obviously, but I soon realised that he wasn't being mean, he had just found a way of getting out of doing things he didn't like or didn't want to take part in. Realising that horses do not think like humans was a lesson in it's self and made me have a good long think about the situation. Despite starting to realise the truth, I soldiered on. I even bought a padded coat to give me some protection when he dumped me. I would get the saddle off the stand and feel dizzy and sick, my mouth was dry and my stomach in a knot. I wanted to cry and I hoped the world might end while tacking up so I didn't have to get on him. I was out of my depth and not a good enough rider to cope with him. Yes, he was very naughty but the problem at this stage was made worse by me being keen but pretty useless on a horse! Yes, see, I said it, I was a passenger, I had no real skill, no understanding and no COM-PETENCE. My keen attitude alone was not enough to get me through.

Eventually I got to the point where I was so scared that I asked a local instructor to ride him in the hope he might mend his ways for them and then me. When he tried his very hardest to get even her off, it was the final straw. She was a good rider and said to me very bluntly, which I hated at the time, "if you don't give up he will really hurt you or worse. He has learned every trick in the book and is not a novice ride". I reluctantly sold him, with a very honest advert to

a young woman who loved his 'quirks' (quirks? Seriously!?). Despite an element of relief, I was still very sad when he went. I was tearful on and off for weeks as I felt like a failure for not persevering and oddly, I felt that I had let him down by not mastering him. He had broken my heart, my dreams, crushed my spirit and to top it all, terrified me. I started to wonder if horses were really my thing and spent a few months licking my wounds. I gave all my riding gear and equipment away swearing I would never get on one again!

It wasn't until I took a dear 30 year old horse on loan with the intention of keeping him as a very large pet that the passion came back and before I knew it, was toying with the idea of riding this poor old dear round the farm. I could have just got on and done it as he was fit for his age and had been lightly hacked throughout his retirement. He had tack so there was no reason not to except for the fact that fear gripped me and I was really struggling, too scared to give it a go and having constant 'discussions' with myself in my head about why I should or shouldn't get on him! As I said though, I am tenacious by nature and I started to work with lists and visualisation. Initially I spent hours thinking about riding this horse, what I didn't at that time realise was the "day dreaming" was in fact a form of positive visualisation. Each time I thought about riding him, I felt more inclined to get on him. Excitement started to bubble to the surface, an inner strength which at the time I thought had come from nowhere! Visualising myself riding this horse around the farm became a nightly ritual when I went to bed. I also started to write lists. They were honest, brutal and made me cry sometimes, I worked through my lists to break them down into manageable areas so I could look at my fears head on. I kept visualising. I had no idea I was re-training my mind turning negatives in to positives and slowly breaking the 'dread-cycle' that I had become stuck in. I started to feel a really strong desire to get on him, I felt excited and I felt

ready to ride him. The butterflies were building, but this time, in a good way, an air of excitement hung over me when I thought about riding this kind old horse.

One night I went to bed and decided that tomorrow was the day I would do it. I was going to ride and nothing was going to stand in my way. I felt supercharged, full of anticipation and wanted it more than anything. It was a quiet sunny evening, early summer, when the evenings are warmer and longer, the sun was low in the sky and that Saturday, on my own, I got on this dear old boy and rode him around the fields in the valley of the farm for about half an hour, on my own. I will never forget it, it changed my life forever and for the better. He gave me my joy back and although he is long gone (he saw his days out with me), I thank him for his mannerly, kind way whenever I think of him. His portrait still hangs on my wall. A reminder of him and what he gave back to me.

Since that sunny evening on my old friend my competence and confidence have grown and I realised that as a result of the former the latter will come. For the last decade with help from my amazing trainer, a traditional horseman with a classical background, who trains horses to the highest level for competition and to do things and go into situations for his work in the film industry as a registered stunt rider and horse trainer. His horses are taught do jobs that most people would only dream of, or perhaps more sensibly, run away from. He has taught me that in any discipline, there is always the need for precision, obedience and consistency and I have gone from strength to strength. I also see now that riding is a journey and not a destination and that however good you are, there is always someone better and there is always room for improvement. Whether training horses for pleasure or competition, his knowledge and skill have been my constant companion. He has taught me the only way to ride is **correctly.** Once I realised there is

no magic, just endless mistakes and corrections, it allowed my riding to progress in to something I can start to be proud of. Now I am riding to a much higher standard I can confidently participate in regular clinics with world class riders from Europe. I have been very fortunate to ride under instruction from these amazing individuals (classical dressage, working equitation and high school) who despite being riding masters and indeed, World and European Champions, are still willing to help the 'normal' rider and unreservedly give their knowledge and tuition to anyone willing to listen, learn and grow.

I have not only competed and continue to do so, but I have also doubled the lead actress on a film which is a far cry from that scared person who wanted to cry getting a saddle off a rack. It can be done, you can change your path. My Instructor has given me time, patience and sometimes a real dressing down, but with his specialist knowledge and supremely high standards of horsemanship, he has pushed me to the maximum. All the top instructors I have been lucky enough to be taught by have shown me that you must find your limit, ride up to it and then you must try to ride beyond it. If I can do it, anyone can.

INTRODUCTION

I hope it rains! Most of you who suffer with nerves, will know exactly why I used 'I hope it rains' as the title for this book. Anyone who has suffered with nerves will wake up on a horse riding day and think 'I hope it rains'. Hoping it rains, in the mind of a nervous rider, the perfect reason (it's not an **excuse**, it's a **reason,** we will come to that later...) not to have to ride their horse.

The relief a downpour can bring is immeasurable to someone who has been worried for days in advance and wakes up on 'riding day' to drizzle. I have been there. I am, thankfully, not nervous now, but knowing how it feels and then how to beat the fear was the reason for this book. I never thought of myself as an author but have come across so many worried riders that I wanted to help. When I was in fear of riding, if it rained, it was as if decision had been made for me and down at the yard I would not have to get on my horse. Also, if it rains, you do not have to confess to your anxiety as many riders will decide not to go out and your cover will not be blown. Nobody will think badly of you because lots of people will decide not to get wet and go tomorrow instead. That is where, currently, you differ from them. They will go tomorrow and hope it's a nice day so they don't miss out two days running. You, on the other hand, will want it to rain again... OK, you could argue that analogy is a little black and white but you get my point.

For the nervous rider, tomorrow does eventually come though. On the day of the downpour the relief is palpable. You maybe even enjoy the day, pottering around with your horse, tidying the yard, clearing out the grooming kit, folding rugs, cleaning tack, knowing that for today at least, you don't have to sit on your [be-

loved] horse. Also, if it dries up later on you still don't have to ride as you 'need to get away' because it is 'too late now' and you can easily remain under the cover of the rain scenario to get out of doing it for another day. To ride today is not an option and this makes you feel relieved, but deep down it makes you very sad and quite possibly angry or even guilty. You love your horse and desire to ride him and so the beating yourself up inwardly begins. Also, tomorrow may be dry and sunny so the panic cycle starts again and this starts to upset you and grind you down. Your mind set becomes locked in a negative cycle of self-doubting, dis-empowering thought which is hard to recognise, hard to admit and hard to break.

There are hundreds of reasons we can find not to ride, but whether it is the rain or the report for Monday morning needs to be written, the kids are playing up or there is house/yard work to be done, the bottom line is this is the way it plays out and I bet you are reading this thinking "oh blimey, that is me". You may want to laugh about it initially, but underneath the 'armour' of humour, understandably, you probably feel really upset and in some way lacking. We love our horses and let's face it, spend a great deal of our money on them. Then to have the pleasure taken away by fear is awful and must be dealt with, as best we can, in order to strike a realistic balance to finally break the negativity and find once again the joy we have seemingly lost.

Perhaps you chastise yourself inwardly as you feel like a 'failure' or 'useless' or maybe it has shocked you that you are not alone feeling like this as there is a possibility you haven't had it spelled out before, let alone admitted it to yourself how you really, **honestly** feel? Either way, you know the relief a drop of rain or other worthy reason can bring and this is the point of this book. To stop the emotional turmoil and be able to get back on track and enjoy riding, to bring back the fun and make you happy in the saddle so that you want to ride as often as you can without any unfounded worries.

Over the years I have read numerous 'self-help' books on the subject of riding amongst others, in the early days, I was hoping to find all the answers, the magic cure and quick fix answer to all my woes. Personally, although I believe they were written with good intentions, they were either a bit 'fluffy' and gave false hope which I could see no way of turning in to a practical solution or they were an essay on psychology, which again, may have been physically correct but I could not see how the lay person could turn this information into practical, every day solutions. I also felt that the ones I had seen never actually addressed the issue of **competence and control of the horse giving the rider confidence.** If you are wishing to know more about the intricate workings of the human psyche, then by all means do read as many books on the subject as you can. They are certainly numerous but I really do question how they can translate their clinical facts into you riding your horse without knowledgeable third party intervention to turn the medical facts in to practice for the average person. As a rider and someone who has researched this subject considerably, the stumbling block has, for me at least, been an inability to put these medical aspects in to a useable format. If you can, that's great but I have tried to write this book for the everyday, for the person who is 'stuck' and wants to help themselves in order to enjoy their horse riding. My other fear with some self-help books is that they give false hope and feed the ego of the author with embellished tales of heroism and literally have no regard for the person suffering.

While on the subject of training, may I take a minute to explain why we do it! It may seem obvious, we train the horse to accept a saddle or harness so that he may carry or pull us for work or more likely nowadays, for pleasure but despite the glaringly obvious a lot of people seem oblivious to the fact they need to ensure the compliance and indeed safety aspect of riding and handling a 600kg animal with it's own mind. Without writing an entire book on horse training, which I feel to a degree is often done sub-

jectively, I do think that modern 'instant gratification, 'quick fix' methods have unfortunately over ridden the traditional values of why we need our beloved horses to be mannerly and responsive to our aids, both on the ground and under saddle and although throughout the book I touch on training, there are numerous books on the subject which are very valuable tools. A lovely passage I once read in a very old military style riding manual is not only lovely, but relevant even today.

"Make much of your horse, ensure he is the most mannerly of mounts. A fool, in order to dupe others, can subdue, bribe and bully him to do cheap tricks or attempt to pacify him to cover up a lack in his education. Teach him correctness in his way of going and train him gymnastically and technically, for the sake of both your pleasure and wellbeing so that if such a day comes whereby you need to sadly pass him on, you have given him the best chance to be loved and cared for by another and given him a future full of hope, where people want to be around him and describe him as a good sort, thus caring for him in his later years, feeling he owes them nothing".

PRESSURE

Before we get in to the exercises headlong, let's look at excuses and reasons. I refer to procrastination, in whatever form it manifests (rain, broken down car, forgetting your riding hat) as a **reason** for not riding rather than an **excuse**. Simply, for nervous riders, it is mostly a case of desperately wanting to ride but the anxiety, worry, nerves, call them what you will, stopping them in their tracks. An excuse is, by my reckoning, something we don't want to do or can't be bothered to attempt, very different to someone who is crippled with nerves and "what if's" not being able to ride. Lets for one moment look at the other people you are exposed to on social media or at the yard, not that their actions should be relevant to you, but invariably as humans, we are affected by the opinion and actions of others resulting in unintentional pressure from our peers and friends. We naturally compare ourselves. In my opinion, social media has its place for building people up but it can also bring us down. 'Friends' posting pictures of 60 mile endurance rides or jumping the wings, galloping along leafy tracks or winning their dressage competitions only increase our feelings of inadequacy. Although we are no doubt pleased for them, and wish them nothing but luck in their horsey pursuits, these constant comparisons can have a detrimental effect. We may not even realise how much we are affected and how much we compare ourselves to others, even those we hardly know and possibly have never met! In the 'old days' we would compare ourselves with people we either looked up to: – our heroes, probably professional riders on TV or more locally with those immediately around us. Now we log on to social media and unwittingly compare ourselves with hundreds if not thousands of people all doing what appear to be amazing things, all the time, on wonderful horses with a sea of rosettes being put on display every day. I'm not saying for one minute that social media is all bad, but take everything with a pinch of salt, remember people only tend to put their horsey triumphs on their pages and a photo is a millisecond in time it isn't necessarily the before and after or in fact, even the truth in some cases. Triumph at competition is great but don't let it define you. Set your own goals with your horse. Enjoy the time you spend on these websites but don't lose track of reality and most importantly, don't let other peoples 'stuff' affect you in a negative way. Limit yourself to how often you check these pages, live your life in the now, in the real world. Let others inspire you to do better but never let these posts take hold of you and get inside your mind as they may eventually get you down, especially if you are feeling low about your riding. Everyone has the right to enjoy their horse in whichever way they choose. Make a note in the course of an evening or day to see how often you end up scrolling through social media, is it too often and are you living your life in a 'fake' world in which everyone appears to have perfect lives/horses? Be aware and control it, don't let it dictate and control you.

So, back to the rain and the nerves: look at the rider at your yard who feels no anxiety or nerves and was probably a bit fed up that it rained. They didn't go out for their ride as they simply didn't want to get soaked. This is the end of their story. There are no hidden feelings, no anxiety, no dilemma, just not wanting to get drenched. Fair enough you might agree? They will ride tomorrow and their cycle continues but is a <u>positive</u> experience. Despite not riding today they accepted the weather and found other things to do. It probably annoyed them a little that they didn't ride but because their general mind-set with riding is positive, it didn't manifest as anything awful that they could not cope with. It simply was a wet day and they went home. It is what it is.

Now let us look at the rider who did go out in the rain. Probably armed with wax jacket, hi-viz and enough waterproof gear to make the army proud, they just did it. They will ride tomorrow and their cycle continues but, again, it is a <u>positive</u> experience. Not worried about a 'little bit of drizzle', off they go into the rain storm and have a lovely ride. I'm guessing that you want to be more like them? Not scared of riding in the wind, rain, past the wheelie bins on bin day, up the busy road, in the sand school 'up the scary end near the mirrors' or across the countryside in wide open spaces? We all know it isn't really about the wet and it could be a number of things but it usually boils down to our mind-set. What we have to do is to unravel the mind-set and find out what has caused it to become negative and weigh up the contributing aspects that make up our mentality in this respect. Be completely honest and look at the whole picture: where competence meets confidence, the balance of which results in our **mentality** as a whole.

In order to understand our mentality or mind-set we must look at it in greater detail which we will do shortly. However, we must also look at the physical and practical reasons behind the *mentality* which are often *capability*. In short, I will refer to this as the competence/confidence equation which we will read about further on in the book as well as looking at ways to overcome the deficit if, indeed, there is one.

WHAT KIND OF NERVES DO YOU HAVE?

Let's look firstly at the rider who rides regularly, doesn't get nervous as a rule but at a show or competition, feels nervous, anxious, has a dry mouth and is excited but is experiencing *similar* feelings to the ones you feel just waking up and knowing you have to drive to the yard on 'ride day'. So, the person at the show feels pretty nervous but they still go in and do the show or jump or dressage or whatever it may be. Feeling apprehensive is NORMAL. It is a reality for most sports men and women who want to do well. It may also be borne out of excitement and passion for the sport or activity. Adrenaline in this form can give the person a competitive edge. Good nerves perhaps!? The mind-set of this rider is 'feel the fear and do it anyway!' It ends up being a fun/good experience and the positive mind-set cycle continues. Over time the more shows, the more hacks out, the more good results, the better they feel prepared both emotionally and physically. Also let's not forget the hours of practice are no doubt improving them and the horse so the whole picture becomes a good one, full of positivity and good results. As Jerry Barber, the famous golfer once said when asked why he was so lucky in competition: "the harder I practice the luckier I get". Says it all really doesn't it? It is also important to realise everyone occasionally has a bad day and knocks a pole down or forgets their dressage test (pity we can't have a sat nav for them) but because the rider is generally in a positive place, they can put the odd mishap down to bad luck and move beyond that moment. It may upset them at the time, we are all human and make errors but the key to carrying on is knowing why it went wrong and trying to not let it happen again. The mind-set stays positive despite the 'blip', the **competence/ confidence equation stays balanced** and everything ends well.

I am sure the nervous rider would be the first to point out that 'anyone would feel nervous at a show' or riding a new horse, tackling a bigger jump course, hacking a youngster for the first time, riding out alone etc and they are right. The difference here is that nervous riders beat themselves up for feeling this way and the person with the pre-performance jitters just gets on and does it, living for the euphoric, happy feeling after they have achieved their goal, however big or small it may be. So, on the drive to the yard on ride day you need to establish if your feelings are the same as the rider at the show. Is it because your 'ride day' is your show, simply because it takes you out of your comfort zone or is there a competence issue here too?

The rider at the show has practiced and feels nervous but is ultimately confident enough in their riding ability to take part in the show/dressage/jumping/hacking, otherwise we assume they would not have entered or attempted the class at that particular level. They would either have practiced more before entering or opted for a smaller challenge or pleasure ride of a shorter distance. Also, looking at fears, nobody would belittle the rider at the show for having pre performance butterflies yet you would inwardly curse yourself for feeling the same way on 'ride day'. We must learn to realise that nerves are normal in unfamiliar or important circumstances where we are out of our comfort zone and not in a 'run of the mill' or definite situation. It is also worth remembering that some adrenalin and a slight nervousness can in fact give an edge to us for clear thinking and good performance. It is the crippling fear that is the enemy, not a few pre-dressage test butterflies which are ultimately borne out of a desire to do well.

I'm not saying that anyone who feels fear driving to the yard on 'ride day' isn't normal, let's get that straight. I am saying that we need to <u>work with</u> and *understand* the feelings so that the butter-flies only appear when we are genuinely out of our comfort zone and also learn how to deal with these feelings and carry on re-gardless until they diminish and gradually disappear. We have to recognise why we are fearful in order to rectify it. We need to make your riding within your comfort zone so that once you are competent enough to do these things your fears move in to the category of 'excited' rather than terrified.

As an example, if you passed your driving test at 17, think back to your first time in your car alone. You had the car, the licence, the insurance and were ready to go. Think back to how it all felt. Did you feel nervous not having the instructor beside you for the first time? Did you think, oh my goodness, I can't reverse into the parking space at work? Did you dread stalling at the traffic lights on your maiden voyage? However it went, if you are honest and look back to it, you probably felt really excited but also nervous the first few times you drove, but as the experience of driving became a daily occurrence, you learned to relax and eventually, now, all these years later, you don't even think about getting be-hind the wheel. Your competence grew and so did your courage. These two things go hand in hand. What scares you can become normal, it just takes time and practice. Practice makes perfect – well, if not perfect, at least more competent!

Take a moment to think about this scenario as an example of scary becoming normal, if you haven't got a licence for a car or motorbike, choose another scenario that first scared you but has now become 'second nature' because you do it all the time and it is just part of every day life. For example, navigating the under-ground stations in London, giving presentations at work, stand-ing up to talk in front of a room full of people etc.

HONESTY

We have looked at why a rider could be nervous or has butterflies at a show but, assuming you are reading this book because it is more than that, let's do the first exercise on the road to sorting this out once and for all. I re-iterate, there are no quick fixes here, it is down to honesty and hard work on your part but you can change your outlook and re-wire your mind-set.

There's no point trying to do this while you are cooking tea, scrolling through social media, playing on the internet or not 100% focussed on the matter in hand. You need to complete this task in four parts and each requires concentration, honesty and patience. So, if you can find a quiet half hour or so, you can begin with step 1. (I know, finding that half an hour may be a challenge in itself but hang in there!)

Step 1. Getting over and establishing the cause of fears

Until you can say this sentence out loud to yourself, you cannot easily progress. Say it, feel it, acknowledge it, "I want to get over my fears but I must establish the cause".

It's not easy to be honest with ourselves sometimes. If you felt awkward even saying that sentence and 'facing up' to it, then that is a step in the right direction. If you cried, felt deflated, silly or didn't feel anything at all, that's ok too. Just go with it for now.

Find a suitable place for soul searching. It may be the garden, indoors at the dining room table or in a comfy chair. Wherever it is, it must be with no distractions. You really need to take this seriously, and not when you are in a hurry or flustered. Take a note pad or four sheets of paper and prepare four columns (or one on each page). This is going to be your workbook in which you explore, analyse and discover the root causes of your problems and come up with solutions. It will be a highly personal piece of self analysis. Until you can be honest with yourself, you will be unable to progress, so really pour your heart out on to the page. It is crucial to be really honest but also very important that you don't get cross with yourself for admitting what upsets you. Don't leave something off or not write it down because if someone else reads it you would feel silly or that you were making a fuss. Nobody else ever needs to see your workbook unless you choose to share it so be honest and write it all down. Every last thing that worries you about your riding should go on to this list. If you have an outpouring of emotion, it doesn't matter, nobody will know anyway, but even if they did, they will not judge you as harshly as you will no doubt judge yourself. Sometimes tears are part of the healing process, they show that you are passionate, that you care and that you want to mend the situation you are currently in. Relax, go with the flow and start writing the first column. You can add to your workbook any time as feelings unravel, but get started with what comes to mind, sit back and let the niggles and worries come to the surface.

Column 1 – What scares me?

Column 1 may include things like the list below. When I did this with my naughty horse, my list was simply one sentence "I am scared to ride my horse because he will throw me off".

- I am scared of my horse on the ground
- I am scared to ride my horse in case he throws me off
- I am scared to hack alone
- I am afraid of falling off
- I am not as skilled as other riders at the yard

- I will fall off and hurt myself
- my horse mucks around on bin day
- my horse is spooky
- I am afraid that people at the yard will laugh at me behind my back if I can't ride well
- I am scared of jumping
- I am scared to go in the arena
- I am scared to hack in a group
- I am scared to go out hacking alone
- I am scared to canter
- I am scared of being bolted with

I cannot say how long your list will be. What I can say is that when you write it all down you must not be worried if it is a couple of things or a whole long list of things. Being honest with yourself at this stage is the key to future success. There are literally thousands of reasons, far too many to list here but hopefully you can describe your problem. If there are multiple problems, you can link together in the next few columns any fears that stem from the same reason, thus creating the problem. Stick with me, I will explain this as we go through.

Column 1 'WHAT' WHAT IT IS THAT SCARES ME	Column 2	Column 3	Column 4
I AM AFRAID TO JUMP A FENCE			

I know it's hard to face up to a fear, let alone write it down, so if you have done that, it's the first step to sorting it out. Be happy with yourself, acknowledge that you have been really brave, you have written down your fear(s) and possibly for the first time, actually faced them. You have taken a positive step to beating your fears and that should mean a big pat on the back for you.

Column 2 – Why does it scare me?

Take a moment to read the list in column 1, but don't dwell on it. Let's look at what causes the initial fear. In the second column write down the detail behind the fear: the 'why'. The reason that the anxiety has started, snowballed out of control and now strikes you with absolute fear when you think about it, let alone try to do the thing that scares you.

For example, if you wrote *'I am scared of jumping my horse'* the detail behind this would be looking at **why** you are afraid, exploring the feelings connected to the fear. Don't just list the obvious things but the real deep-rooted feelings as well. You need to take time on these exercises, dig deep and really think about each problem in turn. If there are several issues, you will have to work through each one separately. This can be done over a period of time, but if possible, try to do as much of your list as you can in one sitting. Be honest, be open and do not feel any shame about your answers and findings.

Column 1 'WHAT' WHAT IT IS THAT SCARES ME?	Column 2 'WHY' WHY DOES IT SCARE ME?	Column 3	Column 4
I AM AFRAID TO JUMP A FENCE	• I will look silly • I should be doing better than I am • I dare not even try in case I look		

	stupid and cant do it • My horse is green so it might jump me out of the saddle or refuse the jump • I will feel inadequate • Who will look after the horse/house/kids if I fall off and get hurt		

To give some examples. I have used one scenario of jumping a horse but of course any problem can be dealt with. *I fear hacking because: I fear schooling in the arena because: I don't like hacking in a group because: I don't want to canter because:*

Answers may be along the lines of:
- I will look silly
- I will hurt myself
- I should be doing better than I am
- I dare not even try in case I look stupid and can't do it
- There might be scary things on a hack like bins or tractors
- My horse is green and gets scared of large vehicles on a hack
- I may not be able to control my horse outside the arena
- I might get lost hacking out
- My horse spooks at the bins
- My horse doesn't go near the dressage arena mirrors or

markers

Whatever it is that you have identified, now put the 'because' in the second column as per the example above. What matters at this early stage is that you are being honest with yourself, facing your emotions and fears and trying to do something constructive about getting past this issue. Turning the negative thoughts in to a positive mind-set which in time will become your general out-look and help find the harmony you so dearly want and of course, DESERVE.

Column 3 - Thinking about the fear and the emotions behind it.

Go through your list in its entirety, take on board what you have written and now do a third column to start to investigate the fear and how it has become an issue for you. Are there factors that link your fears if there is more than one thing that worries you? As I said earlier, we have to look for links to see if there is a com-petence issue or a factor that runs clearly through your problems which, although it manifests in different ways with your riding, actually stems from one or two things but 'leaks' in to many as-pects of your riding.

If your fear is borne of an accident, you will need to really dig deep to work through this issue, but the fact that you have got this far means you must want to succeed. This is a positive and you should be proud of yourself for trying to sort things out.

Column 1 'WHAT' WHAT IT IS THAT SCARES ME?	Column 2 'WHY' WHY DOES IT SCARE ME?	Column 3 Now think about each point in turn	Column 4
I AM AFRAID TO JUMP A FENCE	• Big jumps are overwhelm-ing	Must you jump big jumps straight away, if	

	• I will look silly • I dare not even try in case I look stupid and can't do it • I will feel inadequate • I might fall off	at all? Why will you look silly? Who will think you are silly, Does it matter? Why will you fall off? Is there a skill deficit on your part?	
	• I should be doing better than I am	Allowing peer pressure to get you down? Why do you worry what others think?	
	• My horse is green so it might jump me out of the saddle or re-fuse the jump	Are you making the horse nervy and he is thus refusing to jump or is there a skill deficit?	
	• Who will look after the horse/house/kids if I fall off and get hurt • In my head I want to do it by I can't actually bring myself to try	You could fall, but is it likely provided your skill and the horse you are riding are matched and that you have a hat on etc? Is this because you don't want to do it or that you feel too out of your comfort zone?	

39

The list above is just an example, your own list will be more personal and in depth, but you get the general idea of writing down the initial fear/problem and breaking it down step by step. There is no right or wrong with your lists, just be honest and open minded and go with it. In column 3 you need to look at the problem in some ways as if you are another person looking at your problem from a clearer perspective. Imagine what you would tell someone if your fear was theirs and they had come to you for advice. This may sound odd but you would be surprised how turning the scenario round like this can help to give us clarity.

Column 4 - The Master Plan, working with your findings

In column 4 you can look at ways to rectify issues highlighted in the previous three. Once you have investigated the cause of the fear and looked at what it is about that particular thing that worries you, you will be able to start formulating a plan for conquering it.

Column 1 'WHAT' WHAT IT IS THAT SCARES ME?	Column 2 'WHY' WHY DOES IT SCARE ME?	Column 3 Now think about each point in turn	Column 4 Rectifying problems with the 'master plan'
I AM AFRAID TO JUMP A FENCE	• Big jumps are overwhelming • I will look silly • I dare not even try in case I look stupid and can't do it • I will feel inadequate • I might fall off	Must you jump big jumps straight away, if at all? Why will you look silly? Who will think you are silly, does it matter? Why will you fall off? Is there a skill deficit on your part?	See paragraphs below and list your plan in your own column 4. Remember bite sized chunks lead to progression. Slow, constructive steps will be less likely to overwhelm you.

		• I should be doing better than I am	Allowing peer pressure to get you down? Why do you worry what others think?	
		• My horse is green so it might jump me out of the saddle or re- fuse the jump	Are you making the horse nervy and he is thus refusing to jump or is there a skill deficit?	
		• Who will look after the horse/house/ kids if I fall off and get hurt	You could fall, but is it likely provided your skill and the horse you are riding are matched and that you have a hat on etc?	
		• In my head I want to do it by I can't actually bring myself to try	Is this because you don't want to do it or that you feel too out of your comfort zone?	

Below are common examples of column 4 guidance but the basic content can be adapted to your personal situation (fears). This is the master plan, the recipe for breaking the barriers holding you back and allowing you to move forwards. Like all things where we have become stuck in a rut or feel like we have come up against a brick wall, it will take time to unravel our fears but keep with it and you will be amazed how little steps become enormous leaps when you look back in a few months' time.

I will look silly: think about this, will you really look silly? Who will think you are silly? Why does it matter to you if someone at the yard thinks you can't jump as well or as high as them? Why are they better than you (if they are)? Have they had lots of lessons or a better jumping horse? Is it a fact that their horse is very honest and they can jump big fences because of this rather than because they have any great skill? I have seen many average riders jump an easy, well-trained, honest horse around a set of fair size fences. To the onlooker they appear amazingly talented. However, I have also seen it when these same riders try to get a difficult, young or un-schooled horse over a much smaller jump, often with little success and certainly it didn't look as pretty as when they were on their schoolmaster! I have also come across those who will not even attempt it because they know the illusion of their great skill and equestrian prowess will be shown up for what it is. I'm not saying this is by any means always the case but it is more common than you might think. It is easy to mock others or appear talented when the odds are in your favour but to me, the braver and often better rider is the one who is either slightly fearful but has a go anyway, and/or is on a tricky horse doing their best to school it despite not looking too pretty in the early days. What people have to realise is that if you watch the progress of a genuinely good rider over a period of time, you will see the horse progressing and learning properly. An average or poor rider will at best, on an honest schoolmaster, maintain the status quo because of the good grace and mannerly nature or the horse, or at worst, detrain and sour the good horse, thus making him go backwards in terms of schooling and ruin his good will. Respect should be given to a person who is keen and enthusiastic as a rider but maybe not, yet, as good in terms of skill as they would like but making every effort to have good tuition or improve themselves gradually with correct progressive training. Is this something you can do? It is not about looking silly, but positively addressing our current skill level, working on your shortcomings and ironing out these creases to strive to improve over time. Filling holes in our skill-set is something that most good riders will see as ongoing. There is always someone better or more experienced and there is always the aim of perfection. Do not be afraid to hold your hands up and say "I am a bit wary of jumping/hacking etc, but I am going to fix this with a positive attitude, taking my time and perhaps having lessons and listening to good advice". If you think you look silly because you are trying to do more than you or your horse is capable of at this time then the same applies, try to break it down in to smaller steps. For example, if you put a trot pole down and went over it, then built it up a hole at a time would you still feel as worried? Is it the fear of looking silly to others worrying you more than the actual jump? Dig deep, soul search, try to find the real reasons. Then you can formulate your master plan for beating the negative 'trap' you have fallen in to.

I will hurt myself: Is it purely because you could hurt yourself? In your mind, does this relate, in some part, to looking silly? Maybe if you fall off it is because you are unskilled at the level you are trying to achieve AT PRESENT? That sounds like a strange question but if you weigh up the likelihood of falling off and hurting yourself against the hours you ride it may show you some perspective in terms of statistics. Ok, we have probably nearly all fallen off more than once and it can be part and parcel of horse riding. The key is to have the skill to keep the horse between you and the ground most of the time and the understanding that riding, although enjoyable more often than not, like any outdoor pursuit, does carry a risk factor which we must take into account. We have to try to rationalise our fear to make the joy of riding outweigh the risks. Crossing a road is something we do every day and it certainly carries a risk but you know that by listening, looking both ways and being sensible you go about this daily task in relative safety. You have the common sense and skill to get you across safely. It is the same with the riding, your common sense and skill set will see you through. It is when the competence is lacking that the cracks appear and the confidence takes a hit. Another way of looking at the fear of jumping; trying to jump a 6ft fence with little or no competence or experience on a horse that does not understand the basics or perhaps cannot do that type of athletic jump, would potentially be asking for trouble. Assuming the jump you want to do is commensurate in height to your skill as a rider and your horse's ability then you need to work out if the physical hurt of falling off is the actual problem. For example, is it a practical fear - who will look after the kids/horse/housework if I am injured? Or a more self-conscious fear - I will look silly. As we said, if you are trying to jump a five bar gate and your horse is not schooled to that level and you do not have the capability of leaping over enormous fences then yes, you do run the risk of hurting yourself or your horse and you will no doubt look silly, so don't do it! However, if you strip this back and ride over a small cross pole and educate your horse and teach him the necessary skills to jump a small fence, you can, over time if you want, progress to bigger ones. At the same time you are sensibly safeguarding yourself (as much as you can in any sport) against injury because you are taking it slowly and within your current limits, thereby putting the injury statistic into perspective. You do not have to do puissance on day 1. It is not fair on you or your horse and you are hoping for more than you are capable of at this stage. Do you see how important it is to break it down? Stay safe by doing things correctly and over a progressive period of learning you can vastly reduce your chances of getting in a muddle. Also, it is important that you don't pressurise yourself to the point that you become a failure in your head because the bar you have set is unrealistically high at this stage in your journey. Learn from the feelings behind your emotion and weigh up the competence aspect of the equation. Learn to put the desire to jump a fence in to a bite-size chunk, decide you are going to work your way up from a pole on the ground to raising it one hole at a time over a period of time to one foot or six, whatever you feel is appropriate for you and your horse. It may surprise you by the end of the week, month, year that you have notched up more holes than you ever dreamed possible. The key here also, from a practical stand point is to take your time, get a good instructor if you need to and do not heap pressure on yourself unnecessarily. A hole a week is fine if that is what makes you and your horse happy! The same goes for any area where you are having issues. With the scary end of the dressage arena, build up by schooling at one end and working your way down a little at a time. With hacking out, build it up over time and distance rather than try to ride alone for ten miles while you are fearful, which is almost certainly going to fail and make things worse. Everything is about bite size-chunks and breaking things down into manageable scenarios.

I should be doing better than I am: Beating yourself up mentally and becoming stuck in a cycle of upset, failure and negativity because you want to be doing endurance rides but you don't like hacking around the block can also be borne, like the jumping example, from the competence/confidence equation. We must learn to accept a multi-faceted approach. For example:

1) bite sized 'learning and doing' chunks (small steps, over time with patience, end up becoming big leaps). Look forward not backwards. Feel proud of any progression, however small it may be.

2) good, traditional instructors (emphasis on the word 'good') can be key to helping you improve in a safe way and achieve more than you ever thought possible.

3) riding a suitable mount (or a horse you are prepared to work with come good or bad days) for the type of element you are working at. As the old saying goes 'Horses for courses'.

4) stop worrying what others think, comparing yourself at the yard or on social media and concentrate on being happy with your current situation (acceptance) and knowing that with hard work and determination you can move forward to a better level (ambition).

Patience to hone the skills required for the job you are trying to undertake is key and recognising your ability as a rider along with recognising the capability of your horse is a very important step to successfully managing your fears and expectations. If you are sensible, and the situation handled correctly, it will lead to fewer, or more likely, no nerves at all because you will not be out of your comfort zone, out of your ability zone and therefore, not feeling in any great peril. This is the competence/confidence equation – the balance of both equalling nerve-free riding. Also, think about the benchmark. Did you set it? Is it someone else's standard and deep down you don't really want to do the same as them or is it a genuine benchmark that you are determined to do the same as them? This is a big question because it is so easy to get drawn in to what we think we want because we are exposed to it rather than doing what we are happy doing. If you are trying to do more than you actually want to, no wonder you are uncomfortable. Really think about this factor. Also, are you thinking you should do better because you have had lessons in jumping but despite doing it for years, still only like to jump small fences. What is wrong with that if it makes you happy? What is wrong with Intro or Prelim dressage if it makes you happy? Is hacking around the 1 mile block wrong? Who cares except you? Are you thinking because you have ridden for 20 years you should be more competent? Are you thinking this because you 'did it as a child' you should do it now? I could go on to list every scenario (what a lengthy book!) but break it down into the feelings that affect **you** and try to look at them individually using the list you have already compiled and then apply the Master Plan for getting yourself started on the road to rectifying the current issues.

THE COMPETENCE
CONFIDENCE
EQUATION

Competence v Confidence
– the ultimate balance!

If you are still a bit confused about competence playing a part in how you feel riding, I have a very simple generalised example of how this competence/confidence equation works. An extremely good rider will not be nervous riding a very tricky / spooky / nappy / young / fresh / stubborn / hot / un-schooled 'green' or newly backed horse. **This is simply because they have the SKILLS required to deal with everything the horse throws at them.** Their skill is the key to their confidence. They may not be *happy* with a horse that bolts / bucks / rears etc, but they have the skills to sort out the problem. Although they are more than likely not impressed by and do not want the behaviour to go on un-corrected, they are not nervous. Let's not forget too that a good rider's ability is down to years of hard work, probably plenty of landings on their bum and their tenacious ap-proach under the guidance of the best instructor that they could afford at the time, or in some rarer cases just getting on and doing it, day after day (practice and commitment). They have not found the magic wand of quick fix horseman-ship (sadly, there isn't one!) but just worked really, really hard using traditional, correct, time tested methods, not new fangled, ego-fed rubbish put out by clever marketeers.

So, going back to the naughty/nappy/rearing/spooky or green horse. Let's imagine this same horse with a very nov-ice rider. It is almost certainly going to be a complete dis-aster. The novice rider does not yet have the skills of the experienced rider and the tricky horse is just simply beyond their capability. In fact, the horse is probably going to get them off very quickly or potentially terrify them. This is not because the horse is a demon, it is because he is a horse and he doesn't know until we teach him, what is right or wrong under saddle or in harness and what is acceptable when he is not at leisure in his field or stable. A horse cannot lie. He will always do what he wants until we train and edu-cate him in the most positive, kind, firm and fair way that we can. We must, as riders, know our limits. Over-horsing ourselves is a huge problem. Over playing our hand as a rider is also a huge problem. Be honest, have you got a horse that is too much for your current stage of ability which as much as you love him is actually causing your fears? That might be the toughest question you have had to answer so far but like I had to with the horse that kept depositing me, finding him a new home was the best thing to do in that situation and for both of us, even though that decision was an extremely diffi-cult one to make at the time.

Simply look at the smiley faces below for an at a glance view of this competence / confidence scenario. Where do you fit as a rider? If it isn't a smiley then you must fully evaluate your situation.

NOVICE RIDER – WELL BEHAVED,

WELL TRAINED HORSE   ☺

NOVICE RIDER - NAUGHTY/HOT/GREEN/

UNTRAINED HORSE   ☹

INTERMEDIATE RIDER – WELL BEHAVED,

WELL TRAINED HORSE   ☺

INTERMEDIATE RIDER – NAUGHTY/HOT/

GREEN/UNTRAINED HORSE   ☹

GOOD RIDER – WELL BEHAVED, WELL

TRAINED HORSE   ☺

GOOD RIDER – NAUGHTY/HOT/GREEN/

UNTRAINED HORSE

VERY GOOD RIDER – WELL BEHAVED,

WELLTRAINED HORSE   ☺

VERY GOOD RIDER – NAUGHTY/HOT/GREEN/

UNTRAINED HORSE   ☺

Where do I want to be in the future?

Remember, it may not be where you are now, but it doesn't mean you won't make it in the future, as I said, this is a journey and in time, with practice, things can change.

NOVICE RIDER – WELL BEHAVED, WELL TRAINED HORSE ☺

NOVICE RIDER - NAUGHTY/HOT/ GREEN/UNTRAINED HORSE ☹

INTERMEDIATE RIDER – WELL BEHAVED, WELL TRAINED HORSE ☺

INTERMEDIATE RIDER – NAUGHTY/HOT/ GREEN/UNTRAINED HORSE ☹

GOOD RIDER – WELL BEHAVED, WELL TRAINED HORSE ☺

GOOD RIDER – NAUGHTY/HOT/GREEN/ UNTRINED HORSE ☺

VERY GOOD RIDER – WELL BEHAVED, WELLTRAINED HORSE ☺

VERY GOOD RIDER – NAUGHTY/HOT/ GREEN/UNTRAINED HORSE ☺

There are not necessarily right and wrong answers but you need to be aiming for a smiley face on the examples above, and don't forget this is a moving target. A sad face will turn in to a smiley one later on if you make the right choices and get the right mindset and if necessary, help. Look back in six months and see if the face has changed as you have learned to work within your boundaries and improve your relationship with your horse. Be warned that ego can play a part and that could be your demise. Also, to be blunt, delusion can play a part. You may think you are incredible but in fact, are not! You must be honest with YOURSELF in order to proceed and find peace and success!

If you picked a smiley face from the list you can work through your problems with the lists and techniques in this book, if you didn't and it was a sad face, let's think about what you need to decide: If you are a novice and have a horse that you cannot control (i.e. too hot, green, naughty, etc) then you should consider whether it is worth trying to put a square peg in a round hole. This sounds so very harsh, especially in a self-help book but I vowed to be honest from the start and I stand by that ethic. I told you how despite my efforts my naughty horse had to be sold. It didn't feel like it at the time but it WAS the right thing to do for both our sakes. Having said that, give me that same horse now and I have no doubt I would cope with him and his antics fairly easily. I have broken in and corrected plenty worse than him over the years but the ability to cope is down to my hard work, hours in the saddle and **confidence gained through competence**. I have found time and time again, no matter how these horses are corrected lots of them soon slip back to naughtiness once the less experienced rider gets back on board. **I do not condone selling every horse that challenges you or puts a foot wrong, I despise the culture of 'just get another one' with my entire soul**, but there is a balance to be struck. Therefore, think this through and be honest with yourself. IS YOUR HORSE TOO MUCH FOR YOU? Ultimately only you can decide but if he is, there are options but you need to face up to facts first.

In addition to visualisation and understanding your fears, nothing will entirely replace hard work. When I took up riding again after my 'blip' I tried to do it six days per week most weeks. I know that is not possible for everyone but my point is, do it as much as you can and as well as you can. Keep at it. When something becomes second nature it becomes easier. I reiterate, I do not condone people who sell their horse every time it puts a foot wrong but a persistent offender may need to be exchanged for a more suitable mount for your skill set at this time. Alternatively, if he/she is a beloved homebred or big financial outlay dream horse, could he be ridden and competed by someone else until you get up to scratch or turned away for a short time while you get yourself back on track? The key is to know your limit and then pick who you train with and as you progress re-evaluate the situation. Don't forget, today you may be out of your depth but things change and this does not have to be a forever situation. If you are not progressing consider if it is you, the horse or the instructor which needs to change. You will need to take a step back to evaluate this from an honest perspective. It would be too easy to blame the instructor or the horse. If you are determined to ride well and without fear you must have help at least in the early stages to get you going. If it is a friend on the ground that's fine if you are reasonably competent and just need some support or perhaps, if there are financial constraints, but do not under estimate the progress you can make with the right set of tools. It is entirely up to you but really and truly, if the elements of this book have made you realise your competence level is inadequate or you are very novice, do try to find the funds for a lesson each week with a suitable instructor. They should give you homework so when your next lesson comes around, you have had things to work on and hopefully improved. They can work with you to achieve your goals and carefully set new ones. Make sure they are competent, watch them ride, not only their horse but YOURS. Any instructor worth their fee SHOULD without question, get on your horse and show you what they mean and show you how to do what they are asking you to do. Coupled with the new understanding from lessons and visualisation techniques you can become, in time, with perseverance, a very calm, positive, good rider. Progress is down to very hard work and a good mental attitude to process and overcome obstacles that stand in your way. So, ask yourself: do I need help/instruction?

If you are lucky to have a very well trained, polite, forgiving horse and the fear factor is from a previous accident or incident or even from something you cannot put your finger on, you are possibly, believe it or not, in a good position to progress. As the horse is Ok, it's you that needs the work. In this instance, the lists and visualisation for you is the key and can help iron out nerves and butterflies relatively quickly. You may still need good tuition or a good friend to help you do the physical riding, i.e. encouraging you, hacking out with you or cycling next to you etc, but essentially, if the horse is not to blame in any way, you have half your battle won before you start. Hypnotherapy is a fantastic tool for getting past specific insecurities following a loss in confidence, so in addition to the lists here and working with breaking down our problems, it may be worthwhile to give this a go, especially if you are not progressing as well as you would like. Think of this as a fine tuning method to complement all your hard work with the lists.

I dare not do it at all: Why? Let's think about it. Does it correspond to the previous points? Maybe you dare not do it because social media floods us with people jumping bareback over enormous fences or you see 8 year old kids at the yard jumping 1m 20cm on a pony and feel that as an adult you are in some way inadequate. It is not so much inadequacy at this time in the journey, you are just unskilled or unprepared technically / physically / emotionally and currently unable to complete the task you dream of. However, if trotting poles is your limit then why is that wrong? Just enjoy the trotting poles and don't feel bad about it. The same goes with any aspect of riding, just because you cannot complete a dressage test or a long pleasure or endurance ride right now, maybe in time you will do providing you stick to the plan. Take your time, gradually increase your hacking time until you can go further happily, do some mock dressage with a friend, try some e-dressage and submit it online to ease the pressure. Most importantly, try to laugh when it goes wrong. Build it up over time and progress happily without even knowing it.

Take the pressure away from yourself with bite-sized chunks of learning and progression, fill column 4 with your plans. Make it achievable and although your end result may be a 20 mile endurance ride, jumping the wings or competing at dressage, take it slowly and pay attention to the bite-sized chunks. Walk around the one mile block with a friend next to you on foot/bicycle. Work up to the same block where your friend only goes half way or meets you on your way back, work towards doing it all alone. It will take time so don't pressure yourself but have goals that you are sticking too and can realistically work with. You will be amazed how quickly that single mile becomes 20!

There will be scary things on the hack: Scary to you or to the horse? Are you making him fear something because you think he won't like it? If you are tense and he is looking to you to take him past things and you are not achieving that at present then you need to re-group, visualise yourself riding forward and positively past scary things, not over thinking or judging yourself. Visualisation in this scenario is great for ironing out little creases and subtle problems. Learning to breathe deeply also helps you relax and calms you, so don't rule out this kind of technique which I will discuss later in the book.

By this time next year who knows what you will have achieved. Just don't fall in to the trap that someone else's limit is the same as yours and avoid setting your benchmark based on them. Their competence level may be less than yours in other areas but if it is currently greater than yours and their horse more schooled or physically able than yours at this time then that is fine, don't judge yourself. Just know where you are at now and formulate a plan to move on at your own pace, towards YOUR goals.

SELF PROCLAIMED EXPERTS (SPE'S)

At this point, we must introduce the problem of unhelpful individuals, the armchair horse experts. Sadly a lot of confidence issues I have helped deal with have stemmed, at least in part from other people at the yard or on social media, making comments or being a down right know-it-all!

Yard experts (who are more likely *self proclaimed* experts who we will now refer to as 'SPE's'), that lean over the arena fence shouting instructions, having loud opinions and giving advice, undoubtedly from the safety of the floor, are not helpful and I find the simple "would you be able to get on and show me how to do it" usually results in the horrified 'SPE', suddenly having nothing to say, not having suitable boots, not having their hat with them or 'realising the time' and having to go early today scenario! (Try it, honestly, it will amuse you if nothing else, but it does nip these very unhelpful SPE's in the bud most of the time).

Nobody has the right to criticise or belittle you, even if their 'over the fence' advice is well intentioned, it is usually not constructive or helpful and more about their own fragile ego. The same goes for social media where anyone can pass comment without having to back it up! If someone is offering you advice and they are skilled as a rider and you have witnessed them doing what it is you are trying to achieve, by all means let them help you (obviously you will expect them to show you on your horse – just to be sure they are not one of the blessed few with the school master horse making them look better than they actually are). However, you usually find that a *genuine* helpful person will not be shouting over the fence but quietly approach you and offer their help in a completely different manner.

If someone can help you let them but do ensure you seek the right type of help, not some self serving SPE who is probably not a great rider and dare we say over confident and possibly quite delusional rather than talented in any way. Yes, they may not be nervous but in terms of actual ability, they can usually offer you very little in the way of support, encouragement or wisdom. These overbearing people (you know who they are!) act like wannabe instructors who can kill your confidence in less than a few minutes, so please, BEWARE! OK, so you are smirking now, and yes, I am being a little tough but you get my drift.

However, having picked on the SPE, do not under-estimate the power of groups in a positive way, provided they are made up of kind folk who genuinely want to have fun and grow their skill set together by supporting each other. Don't lose sight of structure and good tuition in these circumstances but laughing and being part of a group can strengthen you. Many yards do 'have a go' days for show jumping, dressage, jump cross, cross country, working equitation, la garrocha, doma vaquera, horse ball and all sorts, so maybe enrol on one of these courses or just get a group of your friends together with their horses at your yard to **encourage** each other. It really can help not trying to cope alone, and having a laugh with (not at) each other is good medicine and a positive experience. Don't rule it out, even if it comes a way down your column 4 list. Laughter and support for one another is a great tonic and you will also realise that everyone has their demons and struggles with certain aspects of riding or have things they don't like doing as much. Once you realise you are not alone in having some reservations, you will start to progress more quickly and see everything from a much brighter perspective.

LOOKING AT YOUR FINDINGS AND WORKING WITH THEM

Having compiled, assessed and evaluated all the columns, you should now be in a position to understand the feelings and the cause of those feelings. You can then formulate a plan of how to progress so that the fear does not win long term. Any fear can be approached in the same way as the jumping/hacking example if you break it down and remember at all times the competence/confidence equation. Find that balance and you will find the way forward.

We now want to look at ways to break down the negative blockages further. For example 'I am scared of jumping my horse' has been broken down in the lists you have made. You have now hopefully opened your mind and your heart to the real causes of the fear. We will assume at this stage that the fear is not because your horse is too much for your skill level and it is either 1) just a 'no good reason' fear that has crept up and you have no idea where it came from but you are suffering because of it. 2) a fear because you had a moment where things didn't go to plan and its now playing on your mind and worrying you or 3) a fear stopping you from doing what you want to do because you haven't done it before/for a long time and it worries you or 4) because you had an accident in the past which haunts you.

We must now look at breaking down the issues even further so that it doesn't seem so daunting. For example, earlier I described gradual approach to jumping starting from a pole on the ground. Or for the hacking fear, starting with a short route with a friend and progressing to a longer ride in company and then alone and so on. If the dressage arena is the problem at the scary end or where the mirrors are, progressively taking the horse up to that end with friends. If you are riding alone, progress over time. Don't allow yourself to get fixated with the issue, thus worrying the horse. Visualisation is a great tool for this and will result in you becoming calmer and more confident each time you ride if it is done properly.

We have established the rider is fearful for the reasons listed. So, let's assume that we can remove the nerves and that the horse and rider are both physically capable of doing their chosen discipline and it is only fear stopping them. What we want to do now is look, in detail at how we approach fear, in a structured format, starting with something small and progressing to a new goal. Once the fear is being dealt with the progression will naturally come and your fear will lessen – and so the competence/confidence equation once again comes in to play. You must take notice of this for if there is a deficit on your part in terms of skill, you are kidding yourself and holding yourself back.

So, along with the strategies we have already listed, here are some practical tips for breaking the barriers physically. We will look at the solution to conquering the problems being dealt with emotionally and physically together as the best way of getting fear dealt with and forgotten moving on to a harmonious riding future. We will also look at ways to enhance the 'recovery' process with Emotional Freedom Techniques (EFT), Hypnotherapy and Positive Visualisation, all of which are extremely powerful tools and should not be overlooked. I had fantastic results with an amazing sports hypnotherapist (Ronnie Hall) who helped me overcome a fear which I felt I had 'for no reason' and although I had managed most of it through the visualisations and lists, he helped me eliminate it once and for all with powerful guided hypnotherapy sessions (I think it was 6 in total). His techniques enabled me to start enjoying competing rather than fearing it. Although a competent rider when I saw him, I still needed to iron out some creases. He was amazing and I recommend people try this type of therapy alongside the other techniques listed here. I found this especially helpful where everything else had been put right by me using the bite-size chunks and small steps approach. Even though I was feeling pretty good about riding, the benefit of the fine tuning really enabled me to 'up my game' and learn to focus and control my emotions to an even greater degree as well as work on controlling the 'good' competition nerves and using them for competitive edge rather than associating them with horror.

A RECAP – SIMPLE, PRACTICAL 'MASTER PLANS'

Jumping: start with trotting poles and over time notch them up off the floor. Perhaps find a FRIEND not 'SPE' to help you if it is the support of another person that gives you more confidence. For jumping ask them to put you on a lead rope and run over a tiny jump with you if that is what gives you confidence to start with, then build it up to going solo over a pole on the ground or bottom hole cross pole. I am sure you will both laugh about it, but in a positive way, not a negative or nasty way. It is very different to hear someone say "oh goodness, my friend had me on a lead rope today going over a pole, it was hilarious". This is funny, positive and accepting the situation as it is rather than the negative "oh, how ridiculous, she had to go on a lead rope, shouldn't be allowed near a horse, stupid woman/man" that is nasty. That person has no place in your life. Try to make fun of your fears. Laughter is a great tonic and smiling heals the soul.

Hacking: build up the ride from a very short one, possibly with an accomplice, to a longer route until you are happy going further and eventually alone. Deciding on small goals can really break down the fear. If you decide to walk the whole way that is fine. You can choose whether to introduce trot and canter once you are more confident. Prepare yourself well by wearing hi-viz clothing and carry your mobile phone with you. Make sure someone knows where you are going. These things give you added peace of mind so you can then focus on the task of hacking, knowing that you can be seen by drivers and have a means of contacting help should you need to.

Scary spooky stuff: for example, bins and things you can move in to your 'world'. Slowly introduce the horse to these by placing one on his route in and out of the yard or back from the school. Just walk past them, don't look at them yourself and very importantly, don't let him look at them or walk him up to them and force them upon him. The damage can be great by letting a horse look at stuff that is scary if you do not have the skill to back up the dislike that he may well show you. While mounted, put your leg on firmly and encourage him forward and past the bin (scary thing) with suitable distance between it and you. By ignoring the 'demon' he is more likely to as well. Try to be brave and he will usually go with your lead. After all, a horse is a herd animal and looks to a matriarch mare or dominant stallion for guidance in the wild so in a domestic situation, you need to be in charge and tell him that it is ok to go past things he is unfamiliar with. The language your horse understands is positivity, consistency and purpose from you as his rider to get him past flappy horrible things that worry him. Don't pat him when he backs off or spooks as you are rewarding him for doing wrong which will confuse him even more, reinforcing bad behaviour with a misguided pat can do a whole lot of damage to any progress you were making. By all means pat him after he has done a grand job and gone past the thing that was worrying him but not on the lead up to it and during it as it creates a scenario that is not necessary and not beneficial to his training. Also, don't forget that the old saying of 'what goes on in the brain goes down the rein' is very true, so do ensure that it is actually the horse that is concerned about the bin or demon object and it's not your preconception of what he might do and your worry being transferred on to him. Using a bin as an example, you can gradually increase the distance you ride from the bin until he (and you) are oblivious to it. Once this is achieved head out around the village on your hack and ignore every bin on the route. The more you stop focussing on the bins, the less the horse will. Talking helps too. If you are alone sing to yourself or recite the alphabet out loud. So what if you feel a bit of a Wally! Talking or singing encourages you to breathe so you stay calm under pressure. Focusing your mind on what you are saying/singing will stop you getting trapped in the moment of horror, holding your breath, tensing or literally freezing with fear. If you are in company, chatting will diffuse the moment and before you know it you have dealt with the bin or scary demon plastic bag and gone forward. Always focus on the next step, not the last one you did – that is past now and will never happen again. Think forward and only forward, your horse will thank you for it and will look to you more and more for guidance and be comforted by your new-found courage. However, do not confuse a subdued or bullied horse for one that is properly trained. These are very different things which are explained extremely well in the book written by the late, great Nuno Olivera in his book Reflections on Equestrian Art.

In the Arena if the mirrors worry you, or there is a scary thing up one end. Gradually ride nearer the object that worries you. Don't make a big issue of it, just circle nearer, increasing your exposure to it. Learn to ignore it by making it part of everyday life.

Book the school at quiet times. No caring yard manager will mind you being there slightly earlier/later than usual to avoid the chaos of the busy times if you explain that you are feeling nervous and want to practice some riding without a big audience as it knocks your confidence. They may even surprise you and offer some help or good counsel once you have given your reasons, in confidence, to them.

Find a good instructor. Remember that not all instructors created are equal. Traditionally an AI (Assistant Instructor) would shadow a fully qualified instructor for a considerable period of time to learn the equine disciplines they wanted to teach before becoming a teacher in their own right. However, it is now widely accepted that an AI can teach unsupervised. This is not to say don't use an AI, of course, if you feel they are right for you and can help with your problem, especially if it is a minor issue, then of course, use them but be mindful that the more senior instructor *ought* to be better placed to deal with more tricky horses/issues. Choosing the wrong instructor can knock your confidence quicker than no instructor so do your homework, watch them teach various levels of rider, listen to how they approach problems and most importantly, watch them ride. Certainly before they take you on as a student, pay them to ride your horse for a session if they will. Yes, it may cost you more than if you were the jockey but it will be worth it as you can see first hand that they can deal with the issue you are struggling with. After all, the proof of the pudding is in the eating! Also, before you commit, speak to them about how you are feeling in an open and honest way. Do not be afraid to speak to several different people until you find the best one for you, someone who can understand you and get on with you. Beware anyone offering you a quick fix or 'new' method. There is very little chance it will work let alone help you and your horse long term.

The great Riding Masters taught in a certain way for one reason only - because it worked. It made the horse fit, supple, obedient to the aids and manoeuvrable, ultimately happy and under-standing of his work. Yes, progression and development occur with new equipment and materials but the basic elements of bridle, bit, reins, saddle, shoes are largely unchanged, and as for the horse? He is completely unchanged! OK, we may not be riding for battle nowadays but we still need a fit, supple and manoeuvrable horse to be able to compete at any discipline from carriage driving to dressage. Being able to put your horse where you want it, on your terms is absolute control and is the key to becoming competent. It could save your life. For example, if a car comes round a bend on your side of the road, and you are in con-trol of your horse, you can easily move him laterally, backwards, forwards out of harms way as required. This really is food for thought. Also as a worthy point which may go against the grain in some circles, do be aware that on the note of qualifications, some of the best instructors I ever had were not formally qualified on paper but hugely qualified in terms of experience. They taught to an exceedingly high level with no-nonsense tuition and limitless skill. Whatever your preference, my advice is do your homework and choose the person who can benefit you the most. They will probably not always say things you want to hear but if someone is teaching honestly and from the heart, it is worth listening to them. Wandering around in all the gear, shouting 'well done' at the top of their lungs isn't always very constructive. Although encouragement is needed in order to progress, fake praise is of no benefit and is usually done to ensure you book another lesson. Good business but bad for the progression of the rider. Another tip, unless the instructor is older (and we should forgive them for not wanting to ride our horse), a younger, fit instructor should really be willing to ride your horse to show you something you are struggling with or to help you get through a problem. If they will not and there is no physical reason why, simply walk away! If they can take your money they should be able to back up their in-struction with demonstration.

When you have found a suitable person to teach you, ask your instructor to help you progress at a steady pace. Explain you have been nervous and although you want to progress and are working on this, you do not want to over stretch yourself and your aim is maybe not to get to the next Olympics but to do a nice polished dressage test or go around a course of jumps for fun and learn to progress as far as you can (or set your own limit, you can always change your mind as and when you feel comfortable). A GOOD instructor will encourage you, help you improve and once you are progressing well, and only then, will take you just outside your comfort zone. You will barely notice, as they will do it carefully and always be mindful of your ability and that of the horse. They will also make the journey of learning fun which will be a cure in itself.

Break your training down into bite sized-chunks, be prepared to feel a little uncomfortable but not in absolute terror. You have taken your first steps and set your goals. You can either put your list of goals somewhere prominent, such as the fridge door, where it will be a constant reminder or, if this overwhelms you, put it somewhere safe and only let yourself look at once a day. That way you may see your progress from a clearer viewpoint.

You are brave and honest, taking the positive steps to become confident, competent and happy as a rider. You have come this far in reading this book so I know you have the tenacity and courage to put the ideas in to practice. You can do it! Refer to the lists you made and stick to them. It does work.

Scary stuff in your mind probably looks like this, but in reality is probably not quite as intense!

A NEGATIVE IN A WORLD OF POSITIVES

We have looked at positives and the last things you expect in a self-help book are negatives but honesty is important so at this point I will promise you a few things: there is no magic cure, there is no special head collar or contraption to make your horse 100% perfect; nobody can cure your fear without you taking responsibility for it and working to resolve the issues. You have to a) want a way forward and b) be prepared to work at achieving your goals. If your fear is because, for example, your horse rears, the fear is borne of the horse's bad behaviour and your inability to deal with the behaviour you must address the problem as a whole. Beating fear can be difficult of course, but through hard work you will conquer it and you will feel a million dollars when you finally do what it is that once scared you. Start to believe in yourself now and learn to work with breaking down the negatives and embrace the positives so that one day it will be just an everyday occurrence that you don't even think about, let alone get worried about beyond the usual evaluation of staying safe and being sensible.

Over the years, the main issues I have dealt with are riders being scared of falling off or the horse being out of control. Obviously nobody really wants to fall off, but at some point, all riders will occasionally do so. The occasional 'involuntary dismount" is par for the course if you sit on a horse and anyone who cannot accept there is a certain risk element to horse riding should consider if their chosen hobby is right for them. I realise that sounds harsh but this is a self-help book and not some fluffy read to make you feel instantly better! Working within realistic scenarios and knowing the truth is paramount and if you cannot accept that occasionally you may come off, maybe don't get on in the first place? What we need to help you achieve is perspective. Is the reason some riders fall off and don't seem to worry, just get up, get back on and carry on with hopefully no injury and just dented pride for a couple of minutes down to not contemplating the 'what if' or is it down to skill? Analyse your reasons, add them to your list and appraise it with total honestly. Are you scared of the 'what if' more than the actual falling off?

Let's look at it another way, a professional rider on a young horse that he is breaking in, may fall off. The skill is knowing why he fell off and how to correct the horse from doing the thing that un-seated him again (correct, progressive training). Acceptance of a certain amount of risk in any chosen sport is necessary but with riding skill accounts for a lot of confidence and the more skill a person has, the less likely they are to have an accident. You must discover if the 'what if fear is manifesting itself because you don't have the skills to deal with the problem in the first place or if it is down to over-thinking the worst case scenario when in fact you are a competent rider and have found yourself bogged down in gloom. Recognising the reason is really positive and a huge step towards dealing with it. This is where the lists help. The lists dig deep and reveal the true answers so you can start to build your positive mind-set.

ENJOYMENT

Setting your goals alone: It can be done, I did it in the beginning in order to get on the old horse, so if you feel you can set your own goals without an instructor or any help, then do so. As long as you feel confident having a go and have broken down your objective into little steps then there is no reason why you need anybody else to assist if you don't want to or cannot afford extra help. However, if the task becomes too much and you find you cannot progress, do not be afraid to ask for help. There is no need to be lonely in this journey so ASK, ASK, ASK! Just ask the right people.

Goals will differ for each person, setting them in steps that suit your pace is the key. We have covered slowly progressing over jumps or doing a small hack around the block or up the track near to the stables before you attempt to go for miles and miles. Doing some dressage in private at a lower level to that which you aspire is more sensible than becoming upset because you cannot complete your Grand Prix test which involves going up the end near the mirrors. Don't over-face yourself, go back to Intro (walk/trot) and enjoy it. Feel the progression as your horse learns to be responsive to your aids, soft in your hand, bending correctly and willing in his steps. Ride across near the mirrors or other spooky things on the arena edge without directly confronting them, use the bin technique where you progressively venture nearer to the spooky thing without marching right up to it and making an issue of it. Time and patience will prevail. This approach is sensible and before you know it you will become at ease with the each small scenario resulting in building the bigger picture over a time scale that suits you and your horse. Don't forget that making each session fun and achievable is the key to beating the nerves which, provided we are riding within our capabilities, over time will help turn all the negatives in to positives.

In the early days, if you really are crippled with nerves, just tacking up and getting on is a step in the right direction so do not let any achievement, however minor it may appear, detract from the fact that you are moving forward in a joyful and positive way. These small positive experiences will inspire you to have another go tomorrow, the next day and the next. Through positive experience, the fear and anxiety will naturally subside because your mind is no longer in a situation where it is associating the task with all those stored up negative emotions which the brain finds hard to process and dispose of. You may have the odd glitch or set back but stick to your guns, keep referring to your lists and push on. You will be amazed how quickly it all starts to come together.

It is important at the end of the session that you feel you have accomplished something, however small. At no point beat yourself up if things do not go entirely to plan, we all have bad days and upsets but look forward and not backwards. Always try to finish on a positive note so that you horse goes back to his stable happy and you feel that you have had some fun and achieved something good. "Rome was not built in a day".

MORE TECHNIQUES TO REINFORCE POSITIVITY

The brain does not cope well with negatives. The human mind, evolved to rationalise, assess and act in different situations can become overloaded, resulting in negative experiences and feelings snowballing. The key here again, is to slowly turn the negatives in to positives and although we still have to think about the confidence/competence equation, the mind can be helped to spring clean and clear out its negative storage areas with a number of positive techniques. See the diagrams below to see how negatives and positives can breed more of the same type of thoughts and become the general mind-set which is great for positives but debilitating for those stuck in the negative phase. See the diagrams to follow which simplify how the brain lets a thought type 'snowball', negative breeding negative and positve breeding positive. It is very difficult to break the negative cycle and this is where the lists and the 'bite size chunk' elements can really help to start turn your mind-set around.

Let's look at some options. These are personal choices. Go with what you know, what you are drawn to, what feels right or what is recommended to you by a friend or something you feel may help just from researching it more if you are unfamiliar with how it works.

These suggestions are completely optional, there are many techniques and systems out there but personally, I have had success with the following so feel ethically, I can only focus on the ones where I have personal experience and most importantly, success.

POSITIVE VISUALISATION

Simply take quiet time, perhaps when you go to bed is ideal as you can do your visualisation before you sleep, allowing your brain to process it over night and without interruption. Visualisation is great because not only is it free, you can do it yourself and fit it in around your life. You do not have to be a guru or an expert to do this, just sit back and give it a go. There are two scenarios to try:- the dream-like perfect scenario and the goal-scenario. For easing yourself in gently, I recommend you start with the dream-like scenario for a few days to accustom your mind to the visualisation process without any negatives creeping in.

Step 1 - The dream scenario

This must be a calm, positive, happy and nice scenario, in a place you feel drawn to, whether real or imaginary. The visualisation can be for as much time as you feel appropriate, there is no right or wrong. You are not judging but witnessing and moving on a journey. You could even write the 'story' down, record it on your phone and play it back to ease the creative process if you struggle with doing the visualisation from scratch. If you do record it, take time to describe your 'story' in detail and ensure you do not rush reading it back to yourself. When you are using it for visualisation purposes it should be slow, deliberate and full of tranquillity.

Here is an example to get you started, add as much detail as you want too, the visualisation should be your own:

Imagine arriving at the stables and seeing your horse in his field or stable, walk over to him, pat and greet him and feel how pleased he is to see you and you him. See yourself calmly grooming him, picking his feet and purposefully tacking him up. It is a beautiful, sunny, calm day with a gentle breeze. You walk to the mounting block or put your foot in the stirrup and mount. You feel relaxed, happy and at peace sitting on your beautiful horse who you love with all your heart. Now, imagine happily and calmly walking out of the stables to a lovely leafy lane, across open fields or down towards a beautiful deserted beach, sun on your skin. Your horse is happy. You can hear his gentle breathing as you go for your ride. The birds are singing and it is a perfect day. The horse is walking along gently and calmly. You are both at one, enjoying your time together, everything is safe and going well, you are able to walk, trot, canter, jump as you wish, you are happy and full of enjoyment....

Be sure in this scenario that you don't let any doubts creep in, that there is nothing to scare either of you and you are so happy, just enjoying the sensation of riding in your dream scenario. Let it play out like a movie in your minds' eye. Always go full circle with your ride. Conclude your dream scenario by visualising you both going home to the yard, dismounting, untacking, washing him off or grooming him and putting him in the field or stable.
The 'route' must be complete from going out to coming home, all the time remaining happy, positive, calm and safe and your perfect scenario. You can make this fit your fear, so for example if the hacking bothers you, tailor your scenario in to a beautiful day with a fun, relaxing hack but for this version of the visualisation, keep it relatively short and light hearted. It doesn't matter if it is a bit fairy-tale like provided you stick to positivity and joy and it covers the basic issues you are dealing with. Each time you do the visualisation (I recommend daily) progress your 'ride' along the dream route, cantering, galloping, jumping, splashing in

the sea, or trotting along the leafy lane. Each day you push your visualisation more and more. I suggest you do this over at least two weeks to get into the rhythm of seeing how nice the visualisation makes you feel and how easy it is to enjoy this part of the process. I cannot stress enough, how much the visualisation must ALWAYS be a positive, calming one in which you and your horse enjoy yourselves and you feel love, laughter, excitement and joy as you are riding along. Always imagine a lovely ride that makes you feel happy without any feelings of upset or fear.

This important 'dream-like' visualisation sets the scene and gets you into visualisation as a technique. As it is a fantasy scenario you should find your mind doesn't wander, allowing nagging negative doubts to creep in. It is of paramount importance that no negatives are allowed any space in this process. Visualisation can be as long or short as you feel comfortable with, but always starting, progressing and ending positively. Your mind may drift, but get back on track as soon as it does. Pick up the visualisation where you were at the point you drifted and carry on. Within a few days you will be able to play the scene out in your mind without too much difficulty. If you fall asleep it doesn't matter, your subconscious mind is still working and taking all the information on board.

Step 2 - the YOU visualisation

Once you have mastered the 'dream' visualisation it is time to take on your problems in greater detail with the YOU visualisation. If you have lots of things that worry you, it will be a case of dealing with them one at a time. Although you can probably cover a couple of problems in one go, do not try to overload yourself by visualising everything at once, build it slowly and set a perfect but realistic scene:– a goal that is achievable. Try to make your visualisation so real it is as if you can touch it. The practice you did over the previous weeks will help you stay on track as you have partly trained your mind to stay with the 'story' and carry out the process. Use the same format as the 'dream' visualisation, stay on track and if you drift, come back as quickly as you can. Your sub conscious mind will be taking it all in, so it is important to recognise that the visualisations must be COMPLETELY positive.

Cover each aspect of your 'ride' in quite a lot of detail and feel each part of the ride as described earlier. Feel the warmth of the sun, hear the sound of the birds, feel the joy of riding and so on. Unlike your fantasy ride though, this one should be a real route you want to ride, a jump you want to jump or a scenario that you want to achieve.

For example, a visualisation for someone who is fearful of riding out on bin day could something along the lines of:

Visualise yourself dressed in your normal riding attire. You are with your horse, he is tacked up and you are going to go for a hack. See clearly the colour outfit you are wearing; the tack you have put on the horse, the horse, see his ears as you sit on him. Now allow your mind to move forward with walking out of the yard, imagine that you are going out of the gate, down the track, and on to the road (adapt as necessary to fit your scenario). *You are hacking along the road, past the cars, past the wheelie bins and refuse bags. You feel the joy of having time out from your day to go for a ride on your beautiful horse. You ride effortlessly and happily past the bins, your horse is ambling along not paying any attention to the bins and he is happy in his work. You carry on down the road to the track, put your horse into a trot, go up the grass track, then ask him for the canter, feel the wind in your face, feel the horse move and feel happy and glad, know that you are in control and can come back to a walk at any time and that your horse is listening to your aids and is obedient and you are confident and competent....*

Again, you need to ride the route as a circle, always come home safely and happily. Do not dwell on the problem, in this case the bins. Note them but see yourself going past them, don't look at them in your scenario, just know they are there but see yourself looking ahead, looking where you are going and getting on with the ride. It is important that you see yourself achieving your goals, not dwelling on the scary parts, even though this is within your visualisation. Even if reality for you presently is horror having to go past bins, go in the school or break in to a canter, remember that all of this preparation is setting you up for success and is part of the getting over your problems and fears. This is the beginning of learning to cope, so enjoy the visualisations and feel the absolute joy of what you are doing; cantering; the route you are taking; getting past the bins or whatever scenario you are working with at the time. Think always of being happy while you are in the saddle, imagine yourself chatting with a friend and laughing or if hacking alone, just enjoying the moment.

Ok, so now some of you are thinking, 'well, yes, it's all very well being super-positive, I can't be hurt in my chair but I can be hurt on my horse!' Yes, you are right. However, anyone getting on a horse must realise that it is a living breathing creature with it's own brain. This is why we **train** them to understand our aids (commands) and make them as safe as we can through their compliance and understanding of what we are asking. As a rider, you will of course occasionally have the odd mishap, but if most of the problem is in your mind, then these are the techniques for starting to work on dissolving the fear and anxiety and replacing the negative 'what if's' with positive 'I can's'. There is no mail order coupon in this book which you can send away for magic glitter dust to sprinkle over you and your horse to make him perfect and you brave, all with no effort. Oh, how I wish there was! So, although there is no quick fix and without hard work, there is a solution for those willing to put in the effort and start believing in themselves.

Keep on track, with your lists, visualisation, instructor or friends, keep in mind the competence confidence equation and always try to keep the balance. Seek the right help and learn to face your fears in a positive and constructive way. There is no shame in going back to basics and working through your issues slowly and surely. Success can only come from repetition and hard work and with some mental gymnastics you can achieve anything you put your mind to!

EMOTIONAL FREEDOM TECHNIQUE/TAPPING

Writing down things that worry us is a well-known therapeutic method. Not only does this outline the fears in black and white but helps us on the way to processing the problem by 'seeing' it and deep down, helping to release the energy connected to this problem. A good Kinesiologist can work further with you on these matters if you need extra help. If you don't feel you want or need other therapies, a good thing to do which his free of charge and works brilliantly alongside our lists and positive mind-set visualisation is EFT tapping. I have found this has helped many riders including myself.

EFT (Emotional Freedom Technique) is a form of psychological acupressure, based on the same energy meridians used in traditional acupuncture to treat physical and emotional problems but with no needles. In a nutshell it is a positive reprogramming technique where you tap on parts of your anatomy with your fingers while repeating aloud, a phrase or mantra and feeling how your emotions change during the course of the process. It is believed this system works by tapping with the tips of the fingers to target the acupuncture points on the face and body where energy is getting stuck or stagnant in order to clear blockages. Energy traveling through these channels can once again flow freely throughout the physical body. It is also believed that doing this when looking in a mirror magnifies the effect. It is a strange feeling at first but the good thing is once you stop feeling self-conscious sitting or standing there tapping yourself and saying your positive affirmation out loud, you can fit this in to the busiest lifestyle.

There are many EFT articles on the internet but most seem to agree that when you have identified an issue you need help with you can tap out the blocked energy in a few easy steps. If you have more than one issue or fear, you can repeat this sequence to address each in turn to reduce or eliminate the intensity of your negative feeling although as with the lists and visualisation, focusing on one problem at a time is likely to enhance your outcome.

Step 1 - Initial feelings on a scale of 1 to 10

Once you have successfully identified the area you want to work on rate it a level on a scale of 1 to 10 (1 being mild, 10 being intense fear). This initial assessment helps you see where you are on an emotional level and will give you something to work from in terms of reducing the intensity. For example, if your fear starts at ten but after using the tapping techniques you feel it has reduced to a five it is a significant improvement. Over a period of time the level of intensity of the negative feeling should diminish meaning that the fear has been suitably dealt with and significantly diminished or been eradicated completely. Providing the competence/confidence equation has been addressed and is balanced, the tapping programme can help you reinforce your positive mind-set and help you break free from your emotional stresses and go forward in life.

Step 2 - Setting up your mantra

So, you are ready to start working on the tapping, you have established your fear or issue and now you need to make up a simple phrase (mantra) that will help you acknowledge the fear and accept yourself despite the issue you are facing. The one I believe is a common setup phrase is: "Even though I (insert fear or problem), I deeply and completely love and accept myself anyway." After a couple of days of this, introduce a positive 'next step' mantra – something along the lines of "I choose to enjoy (insert fear – i.e. hacking, jumping, schooling near the mirrors!)"

Step 3- The actual tapping sequence

The EFT tapping sequence is the methodical tapping of your fingers on the acupressure points. I usually tap five times at each point whilst saying my mantra. This teaches us to be in charge of our own mind and create our own outlook.

Although there are twelve meridians the EFT technique focuses on these nine:

- karate chop (small intestine meridian)
- top of your head (the governing vessel)
- eyebrow (the bladder)
- side of the eye (gallbladder)
- under the eye (stomach)
- under the nose (governing vessel)
- chin (central vessel)
- Just under the collarbone (kidneys)
- under the arm (spleen)

Begin by tapping the karate chop point on your hands while simultaneously reciting your mantra, then tap each following point five times with your finger tips, moving through the points in this order:

- inner edge of eyebrow

- side of the eye
- under the eye in the centre
- under the nose in the centre
- chin in the centre
- just under the collarbone
- under the armpit
- finish on the top of the head in the centre
- 'karate chop' your hand

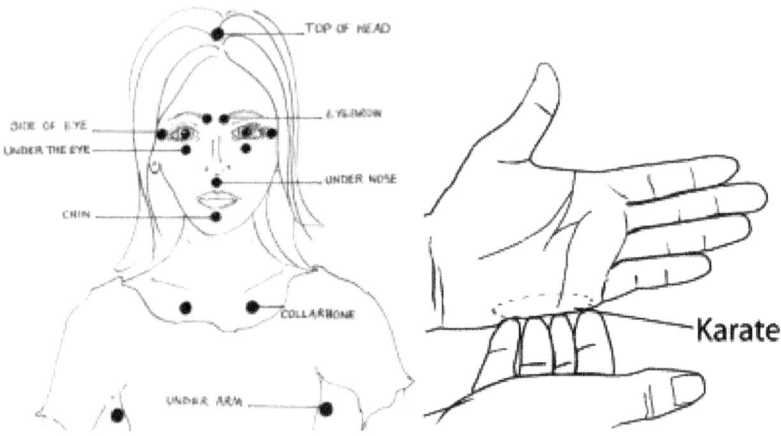

4. Rate your fear

After doing the tapping a couple of times, rate the intensity of the fear as you feel it now. Compare your results with your initial intensity level. If you haven't reached 0, repeat this process until you feel the intensity is lower than it was (zero is ideal but 1 or 2 is acceptable). You will notice that over time the fear will subside. This is a great technique for dealing with fears and although at first appears slightly strange, is a powerful tool to have in your repertoire. I found that tapping several times a day over the course of a month made the most difference to me personally but of course, everyone will respond differently.

Another tip is write your positive affirmation on a sticky note and pin it to your mirror in the bedroom so you can read it before bed and when you get up. Take every opportunity you can to embed this positive mind-set in your life!

KINESIOLOGY

Another powerful tool to consider is Kinesiology. The study of mental issues and blocks as well as physical performance, emotional function and all round wellbeing. A qualified Kinesiologist will use a non-invasive system of muscle response testing to identify and eliminate mental and physical problems. It is probably more associated with allergy testing but Kinesiology is a powerful tool for helping you re-set your mental and physical balance.

It is purported that people can benefit from Kinesiology in a number of ways, including:

- Enhanced learning abilities.
- Improved sports performance.
- Eliminating emotional, physical and mental stress.
- Assisting with decision-making.
- Overcoming past trauma.
- Identifying nutritional excess or deficiency.
- Aiding in muscle injury healing.
- Releasing fears and phobias.

I have used Kinesiology for a number of years and it has definitely enhanced my wellbeing on many occasions. I have successfully cleared emotional blockages and it has helped me with confidence, stress, diet and nutrition and identified a number of health issues. I would recommend this to anyone who is in need of a boost. Also, it works extremely well with our lists and EFT tapping so all these processes combined can help achieve your goals, especially when you have worked to iron out many of the creases but still have a minor blockage that you need help to overcome. Many Progressive Kinesiologists will use EFT Tapping so if you are unsure, maybe book a single session so they can guide you initially. Everyone will teach their own method but do what feels right and works for you.

Thought cycles can easily trap you in a mind-set which then becomes your general outlook. Positivity breeds positivity whilst negative thoughts breed more negativity. EFT tapping, meditation, hypnotherapy and other practices which help you overcome your negative feelings and turn them in to positives are not to be under estimated. They can help you over the little stumbling blocks that are holding you back and stopping you doing things you want to do or being the best you can be.

CONCLUSION

Given that each person is different, there will always be systems that work for one person and not another, but having used the techniques in this book on myself and with a number of nervous riders, I feel passionately that it can help many others which is my one and only aim. There is a sea of confusion out there in the horse world when it comes to training and I hope that I have shed some light on what to look for in terms of instruction, correct riding and the journey to make you a better rider and your horse a mannerly, pleasurable mount who is **happy** in his work.

Yes, of course, there are elements which you have to understand and come to terms with in order for the system to work effectively, which of course is sometimes difficult, but you need to understand if you choose to ignore the facts you will get watered down results. Although this choice is yours and forms part of the rich tapestry of learning, in life you must be realistic and wise beyond your emotions which is not an easy task. It is often much easier to criticise others than look at where we are not hitting the mark and facing up to our issues can be very upsetting and a little bit daunting at times. There will be good days and bad days along this journey but it is these ups and downs that make you a stronger person, more able to understand your horse, a better rider in the long term and hopefully, very importantly, a lot happier! Anyone who understands the passion of my eight year old self with the jumble sale riding hat deserves to sit on their horse without fear. I have through my own journey, tried to make that a reality and through this book help you achieve your dreams too.   There is an element of face your fears and do it anyway, but with this system, I found that it worked time and time again, not just for major issues but for ironing out little creases in life as and when they appear. Determination and honesty were key to unlocking my potential and I hope it helps you unlock yours.

SOMETHING TO
TOUCH YOUR SOUL

"When I bestride him, I soar.
I am a hawk: he trots the air;

the earth sings when he touches it;

the basest horn of his hoof is more musical

than the pipe of Hermes"

*- **William Shakespeare***

A HORSE'S PETITION TO HIS MASTER

Going up hill, whip me not,

Going down hill, hurry me not,

On level ground, spare me not,

Of hay and corn, rob me not,

Of pure water, stint me not,

Tired or hot, wash me not,

Sick or cold, chill me not,

With bit and reins, jerk me not,

When you are vexed, strike me not,

When old and grey, despise me not,

When past my labour, work me not,

When sick and dying, leave me not,

And when I am gone -

FORGET ME NOT

Author unknown.

CREDITS AND RESOURCES

Ronnie Hall – Sports Performance Hypnotherapy, Suffolk. For helping me fine tune my competitive self. www.ronniehall-hypnotherapist-suffolk-essex.co.uk

Sarah Cameron – editing and removal of exclamation marks for which I am so very grateful!

AB Film Horses – cover picture and wheelie bin picture. www.abfilmhorses.co.uk

Sarah Rayner – for helping me heal myself. The Kinesiology Federation UK

Elizabeth Ebsworth, Tanya Simpson, Wolf James Photography Studios

DEDICATION

Andy Butcher (AB Equitation in Suffolk), for being a great horseman, fantastic horse trainer and one of the few who can make a horse truly dance. You are an inspirational, tough, no nonsense instructor and I appreciate your support from walk to passage!

To Shaky, Prince, Sunny, Dublin, Polly, Hazel, Charlie, Tenko, Dear Patch, Vienna, Tubby (aka Dubya G), Darling Flurry (Fluffy), Squirt, Rusty, Cohetta, Kalashnikov, Billy, Vaquera, Divatido and my beautiful, talented Helicon (aka King Zippy) for everything you taught me and continue to give me.

To Bluebell, Weena Dog, Roxy & Bailey for your loyalty. To Alf for being unique.

To Hannah Ellis for your constant kindness.

And.....

to a battered old velvet riding hat for teaching me to always follow my dreams!

ABOUT THE AUTHOR

Born in 1973 I grew up in a small town called Oulton Broad in Suffolk. As a young girl, I was desperate to ride horses but not allowed. In hindsight, it just was never going to happen but at the time I had no clue that my persistence wouldn't pay off and continued to pester my very non-horsey parents, oblivious to the fact that I wouldn't actually learn to ride until I was in my early twenties.

I remember on holiday one year trying to persuade them that if I couldn't have a horse, I would settle for a donkey! My quest for horses was unwavering, I was getting no nearer the actual horse part of my desire, but to appease me, and in a respectful kindness to my obsession (which apparently I would grow out of....) every birthday or Christmas there was always another book on equines and the latest plastic horse for my dolls house or for Barbie. I was no nearer to my dream of sitting on these magical creatures but in order to be near horses I would cycle miles from my house to go and see any I could in their fields on the marshland paddocks despite being told not to go that far from home. I used to pick grass and offer it over the barbed wire fences in the hope that one or two of these fantastic creatures would wander over so I could smell them, stroke their necks.

Despite not riding, aged about 8, I went to a jumble sale with my mum and best friend and spent all my pocket money on a very old black velvet riding hat. To me it was the most beautiful thing in the world and a step closer to my dream of riding. It smelt funny, it was a worn out but still had the

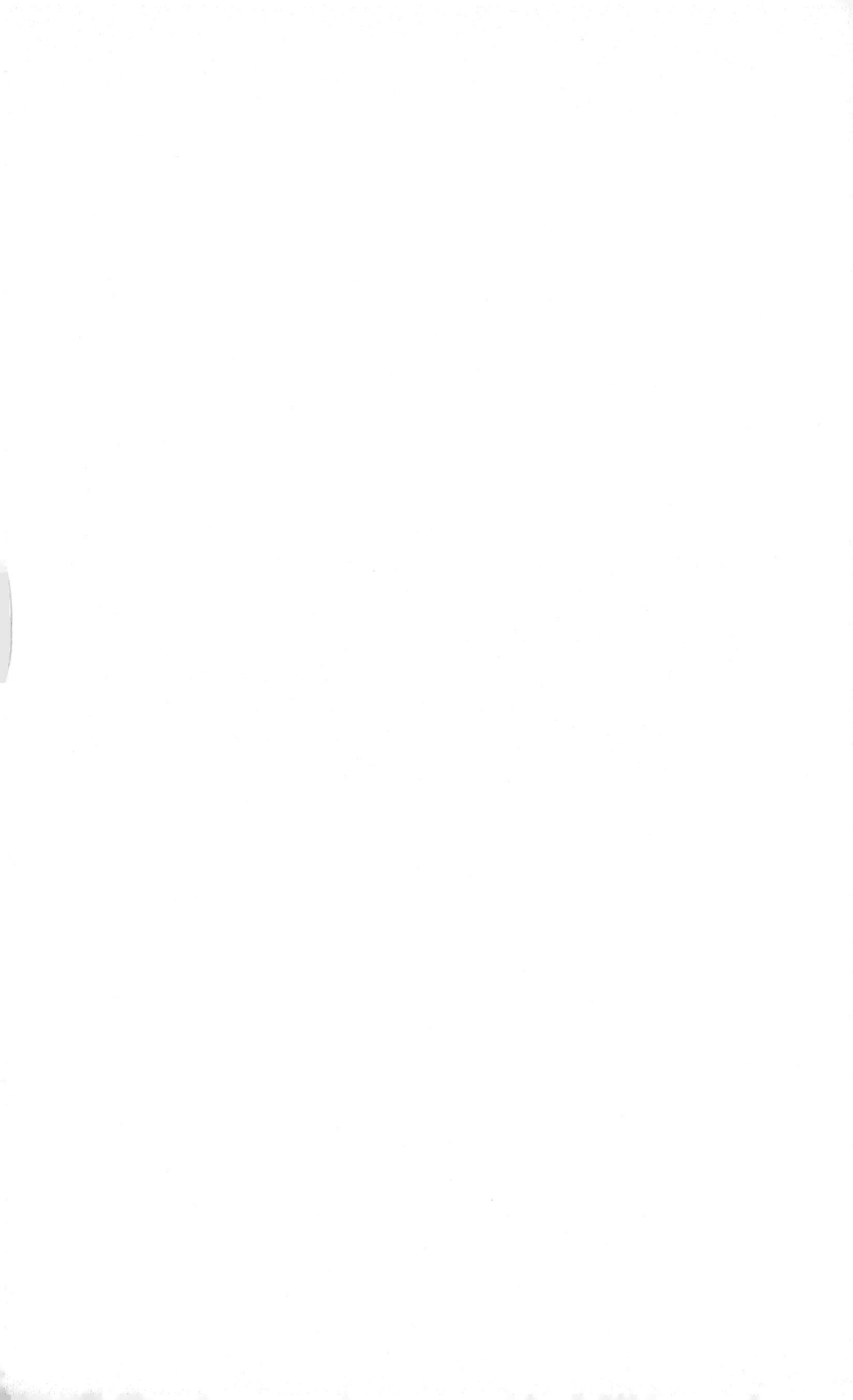

shiny black velvet with a dark purple silk lining, and an elastic chin strap (I kid you not!). I wore it in the house, I hung it on my handlebars to make it look as if I was going off to the stables when I played out on my bike. I was obsessed. I still am!

My passion never left me but eventually dreams of horses gave way to moving to Norwich, high school, exams , jobs and boyfriends. At the point when my parents probably would have let me ride, life as an older teenager didn't, ironically, seem to have time for any of it! It wasn't until I moved out as a 21 year old to a more rural area that I found there were paddocks at the bottom of the lane which had three gorgeous horses in them. I would walk my dear German Shepherd Zara up to see the horses and in no time the passion bubbled back to the surface once again. With no clue and armed only with enthusiasm I approached the owner and asked if she would teach me to ride. She thankfully said yes (thank you Linda). There is another book in itself from that point on, and I can assure you it wasn't all plain sailing, but without the ups and downs THIS book would not exist! I now have my own yard, feel confident and competent with horses both mounted and on the ground. I have completed over 1500 recorded distance riding miles, drag hunted, hacked, jumped, shown and 'dressaged' my way through my horsey life thus far. I have also introduced my young horse to working equitation, which I continue to study. I live for my three beautiful horses and each day remain thankful for the lessons they teach me and the joy that just seeing them over the stable door brings to my head, my heart and my soul.

Printed in Great Britain
by Amazon